Andre Eduardo Menegasso

NoSQL

Andre Eduardo Menegasso

NoSQL

A comparison between relational and non-relational (noSQL) DBs

ScienciaScripts

Imprint
Any brand names and product names mentioned in this book are subject to trademark, brand or patent protection and are trademarks or registered trademarks of their respective holders. The use of brand names, product names, common names, trade names, product descriptions etc. even without a particular marking in this work is in no way to be construed to mean that such names may be regarded as unrestricted in respect of trademark and brand protection legislation and could thus be used by anyone.

Cover image: www.ingimage.com

This book is a translation from the original published under ISBN 978-620-2-18179-2.

Publisher:
Sciencia Scripts
is a trademark of
Dodo Books Indian Ocean Ltd. and OmniScriptum S.R.L publishing group

120 High Road, East Finchley, London, N2 9ED, United Kingdom
Str. Armeneasca 28/1, office 1, Chisinau MD-2012, Republic of Moldova, Europe
Printed at: see last page
ISBN: 978-620-7-31885-8

FEDERAL TECHNOLOGICAL UNIVERSITY OF PARANÁ - UTFPR SPECIALIZED COURSE
IN DATABASE, ADMINISTRATION AND DEVELOPMENT

ANDRÉ EDUARDO MENEGASSO

STRUCTURAL COMPARISON OF RELATIONAL DATABASES AND NON-RELATIONAL DATABASES (NOSQL)

SPECIALIZED MONOGRAPH
ANDRÉ EDUARDO MENEGASSO

MEDIANEIRA
2013

1

STRUCTURAL COMPARISON OF RELATIONAL DATABASES AND NON-RELATIONAL DATABASES (NOSQL)

> Diploma work presented to the Diploma Work discipline, of the Specialization Course in Database, Administration and Development - DIRPPG - of the Federal Technological University of Paraná - UTFPR, as a partial requirement for obtaining the title of Specialist.
>
> Advisor: Prof. MSc. Fernando Schütz

Ministry of Education
Federal Technological University of Paraná
Directorate of Research and Post-Graduation of the
Specialization Course
in Database, Management and
Development

TERM OF APPROVAL

STRUCTURAL COMPARISON OF RELATIONAL DATABASES AND NON-RELATIONAL DATABASES (NOSQL)

By

André Eduardo Menegasso

This Diploma Paper (DT) was presented at 9:30 a.m. on June 26, 2013 as a partial requirement for obtaining the title of Specialist in Database Postgraduate Studies at the Federal Technological University of Paraná, Medianeira *Campus*. The student was examined by the Board of Examiners made up of the undersigned professors. After deliberation, the Board of Examiners considered the work approved with praise and merit.

Prof. MSc. Fernando Schutz UTFPR - Medianeira Prof. Dr. Claudio Leones Bazzi UTFPR - Campus   Medianeira Campus

Prof. MSc. Ricardo Sobjak
UTFPR - Medianeira Campus

SUMMARY

MENEGASSO, André Eduardo. Structural Comparison of Relational Databases and Non-Relational Databases (NOSQL). Final Paper (Specialized Course in Database Management and Development). Federal Technological University of Paraná. Medianeira, 2013.

Databases can be considered the foundation of today's systems. Every system needs a database to work properly and to guarantee the best performance by choosing the right one.
The aim of this work is to make a comparative analysis of the database management systems (DBMS) MySql and MongoDB, showing the characteristics of each, in relation to the basic concepts and their evolution, and demonstrating their particularities through an experimental study.

Keywords: Database, NoSQL, MongoDB, MySQL, Morphia, Hibernate.

TABLE OF CONTENTS

1   INTRODUCTION

Nowadays, databases are becoming increasingly important in the development of applications in general. They can be considered the backbone of the main systems developed.

Not least the choice of a database management system and the database itself must be critically studied in all its aspects and characteristics until the best option for use is found.

In this way, the database is fundamental to the performance of the system in question, making the success of an application or its failure. The purpose of this study is to prioritize the study of a database model called NoSQL *(Not Only Sql),* which should be discussed in stages along with other comparative databases in order to deepen knowledge in this area.

In addition, a case study will be done with MongoDB and MySql, in which some of the main differences between them will be shown, demonstrating the particularities of each.

1.1   GENERAL OBJECTIVE

Compare the performance of MongoDB and MySql databases and create an application with a relational model and a document-oriented model to exemplify this new market technology.

1.2   SPECIFIC OBJECTIVES

Describe relational and non-relational database concepts.

Compare the performance of databases and their specific types.

Create a system to exemplify the use of technologies emphasizing MongoDB and MySql as a database.

1.3   BACKGROUND

Choosing a database is important for any system, as it is a decision that needs to be made very carefully so that there are no inconformities in the future. The point is that when a database is chosen, it needs to be prepared to support a high number of users and operations being carried out all the time. This means that the wrong decision has an impact on the malfunctioning of the systems, as well as on the cost that a bad choice can generate.

In this aspect of choosing the right database to create an application, it is essential to have an overview of how these databases work. Various technologies will be used to develop this work, which involves comparing different structures. This will make it possible to evaluate the best option for use in systems from different segments.

MongoDB and MySQL are the main databases used here to compare these databases with different types of mappings. The result will be an analysis of their performance, giving a broad panorama of knowledge to those who use the work for research and learning.

1.4   WORK STRUCTURE

The work is divided into five chapters, the first of which gives an overview of the work, presenting a brief introduction to what will be discussed. This is followed by a theoretical framework, showing the many concepts of databases. The third and fourth chapters present the methods used to create the project and the results generated from this point onwards. Finally, the final considerations present an overview of the monograph.

2   LITERATURE REVIEW

This chapter presents a review of the literature on the subject.

2.1   DATABASES

According to Heuser (2004) a database represents a set of data that are integrated with the aim of serving a community of users as well as storing data for future retrieval on a small, medium or large scale.

In this respect, a database must be carefully managed, and the Database Management System (DBMS) comes into play. According to Korth (1999), a DBMS is made up of a set of data associated with a set of programs for accessing this data, the main purpose of such a program being to provide a convenient and efficient environment for retrieving and storing database information.

2.1.1   SQL language

According to Silva and Oliveira (2005), SQL *(Structured Query Language)* was created in the mid-1970s and has become a standard language for relational databases because it is easy to use. The language consists of a set of instructions for manipulating data.

There are three types of subset of languages for executing restricted functions, according to Machado and Abreu (2004), which are Data Definition (DDL), Data Manipulation (DML) and Access Control (DCL).

2.1.2   Data model

A (database) model should be understood as a description of the types of information that are stored in a database, and can also be understood as a formal description of the structure of a database (HEUSER, 2004).

To create a data model, there are conceptual creation tools that are used for data description, relationships between data, data semantics and consistency rules.

2.1.3 Relational logic model

The logical database model should be understood as the data model that represents the data structure of a database as seen by the DBMS user (HEUSER, 2004).

The relational model is the logical representation of data that allows you to have relationships between all the data and can be represented by a set of tables, entities, relationships, attributes, cardinalities and other methods.

According to Korth (1999) a relational model can be defined as:

> "The relational data model is based on a collection of tables. The database user may wish to query these tables, inserting new tuples, deleting tuples and updating (modifying) tuples. There are many languages for expressing these operations."

In this context, you can understand what the logic around the relational model is made up of, with aspects built for a database and for users to query via SQL.

2.1.4 Entity-relational model

The Entity Relational Model (ER) is based on the perception that the real world is made up of objects called entities and the set of relationships between them. It was developed to facilitate database design, allowing the study of what will be implemented in the logical system. There are three main foundations to this model: Entities, Relationships and Attributes (KORT, 1999).

Entities can be thought of as "objects" in the real world, where they are interconnected to form a real context for any situation or business rule to be applied to the management or creation of a database. Relationships are the associations made between entities. Entities can have one or more interconnections with symbols representing the language. Attributes are values that describe the entity, in other words, they are the characteristics of that same class (MACHADO; ABREU, 2004).

An example of this model is shown in Figure 1.

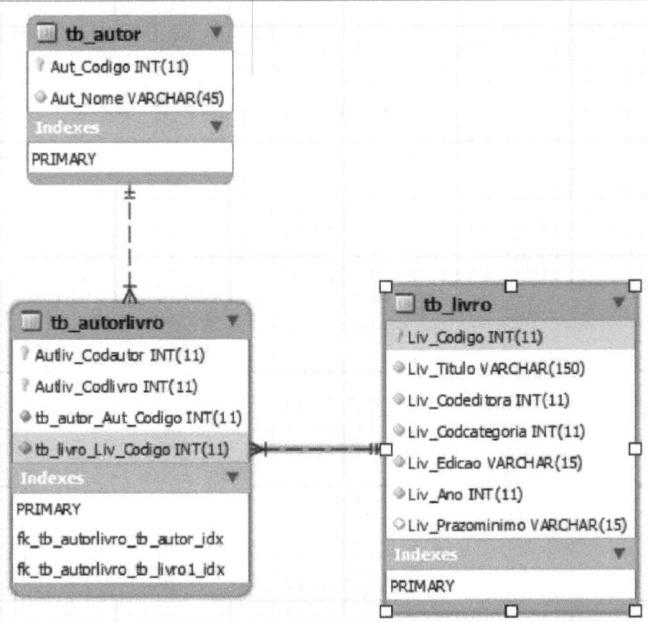

Figure 1 - Entity Relationship Modeling.

With this model we can analyze an example of a MER generated by the SQL Developer function using the MySQL Workbench tool. It is a simple example of creating a database containing three tables where there are two tables "TB_BOOK - TB_AUTHOR", and an associative table "TB_AUTHORBOOK". This example also shows the attributes of each table and their relationships, demonstrating the interconnections between them.

2.1.4   ACID properties

DBMSs aim to ensure that their operations are transacted with guarantees in the databases used. To this end, some rules have been created called ACID, which in turn is an acronym for Atomicity, Consistency, Isolation and Durability, Roman et al (2002) defines these rules as:

- Atomicity: The ability of a transaction to have all its operations executed together and packaged. Atomicity ensures that options are executed with an "all or nothing" paradigm;

- Consistency: ensures that after a transaction is completed, the system state is consistent;

- Isolation: this rule prevents transactions made simultaneously from seeing each other's incomplete results. Thus, each transaction is isolated, allowing several transactions to be recorded in the bank without knowing each other, as each one has its own restricted isolation;

- Durability: ensures that confirmed resource updates become permanent, surviving failures such as machine crashes, power outages, network outages, disk outages and so on;

2.2   DIAGRAM CASE TOOLS FOR MODELING

There are several tools for creating ER (Entity Relationship) modeling diagrams. These are used to model database diagrams and are very useful for this important role of analyzing and creating databases:

Workbench is part of the MySql database package created by Oracle Corporation, which allows a DBA, developer or data architect to design, model, generate and manage databases. It includes an ER modeler, provides other fundamental resources for modeling and executing data, and the tool is free (ORACLE, 2013). Application shown in Figure 2.

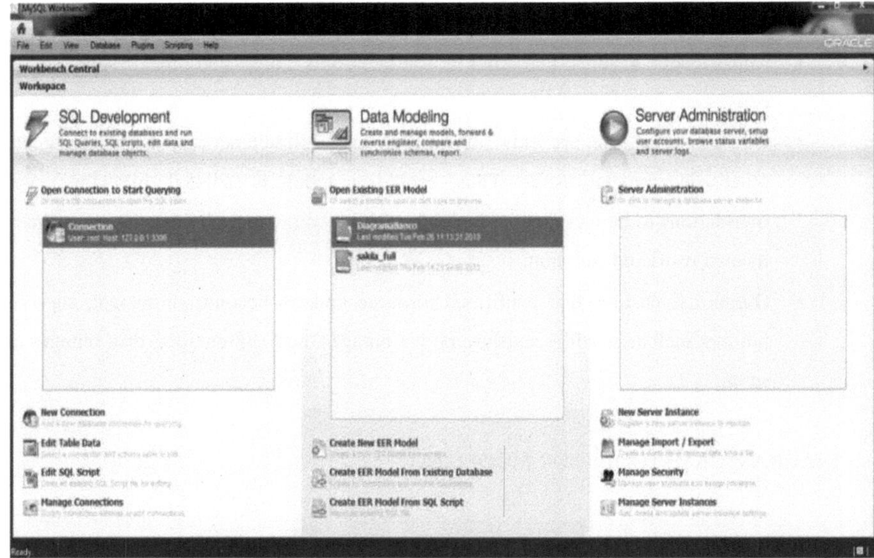

Figure 2 - Workbench environment.

Another tool that provides resources for complex modeling is the free Astah Community software, available at: <http://astah.net/editions/community>. This is a specific UML creation tool, but it allows you to create ER diagrams as seen in the example in Figure 3.

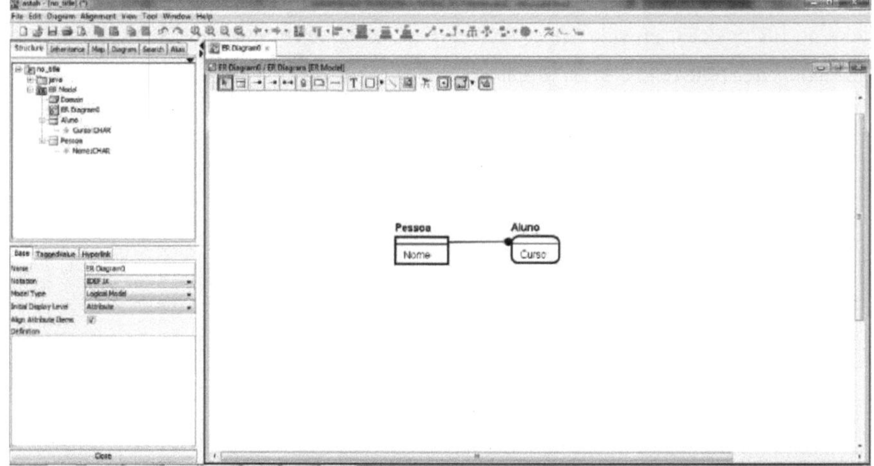

Figure 3 - Astah program for ER modeling.

2.3   MYSQL DATABASE

MySQL software offers fast, multi-threaded, multi-user development and a robust SQL Server database, which is a registered trademark of Oracle Corporation.

Main features of MySQL by MYSQL (2013):

1. Portability:

   - Written in C and C++;
   - It works on several platforms;
   - Designed to be multi-threaded, to easily use multiple CPUs;
   - It provides transactional and non-transactional mechanisms;

2. Support and tools

   - Support for several languages;
   - Support for character sets and the Unicode standard.
   - It includes various utility programs such as MySQLdump and MySQLadmin and graphical interfaces such as MySQL Workbench.

2.3.1 Oracle Corporation

Oracle Corporation is a company that provides the world's most complex, open and integrated enterprise software and hardware systems (ORACLE, 2013).

The company has many segments, including its own ERP, EBS as it is called, which includes various modules and associated programs, as well as its own database. Oracle also has free software projects for the academic community.

2.3.2 MySQL Security and Scalability

MySQL has a very flexible, secure password and privilege system that allows host-based verification. This allows access to the database to be much more secure in any application that uses it. The password is encrypted when a station is accessing the database (MYSQL, 2013).

Scalability can be understood as the capacity of the infrastructure to meet a growing demand for use. This is achieved by optimizing resources in order to extract the highest performance from software and machines.

The MySQL server has a structure that supports large databases, with up to 50 million disks, 200,000 tables and 5 billion rows (IMASTERS, 2013).

2.4   OBJECT-RELATIONAL MAPPING

According to Coelho and Sartorelli (2004), Object-Relational Mapping (ORM) is the act of converting objects in memory into relational data, i.e. it is a technique for translating a relational schema into an object model.

The scheme for saving data in the database using the Object Oriented model and using SQL to save it in the database, this scheme is called data persistence and is a way of ensuring that the data is persisted in the database.

Data persistence is done through object-oriented programming and can be programmed in various IDEs. After creating the code in these tools, persistence is done automatically by generating SQL code for the relational model and the database, the recording is shown in Figure 4.

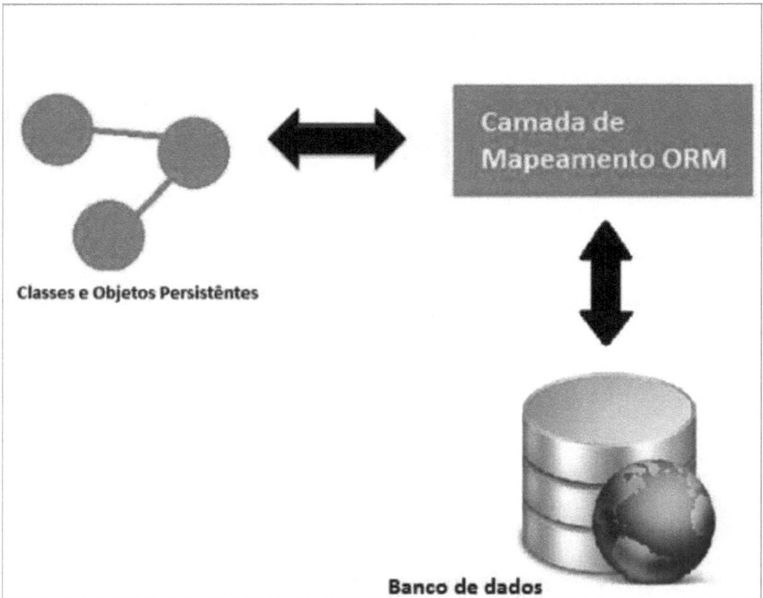

Figure 4 - Object-Relational Persistence Schema.

In figure 4, the spheres are the persistent classes and objects created in any compiler. These classes and objects are references to real-world logic. The mapping layer is provided by frameworks (mentioned in the next subchapter) that manage the connection via an XML file, after which the data is persisted in a database. Mapping is the middle ground that makes connections between the database and the persistent objects, with or without feedback from both sides.

In order to build object-oriented applications and relational databases, a technique called Object-Relational Mapping must be used.

Frameworks to carry out this process have been developed and are described in the following sections.

2.4.1 Hibernate

Hibernate makes use of persistent objects commonly known as POJO *(Plain Old Java Object)* to mediate between the application and the XML used, bridging this same XML with the database, all of which can be seen in Figure 5.

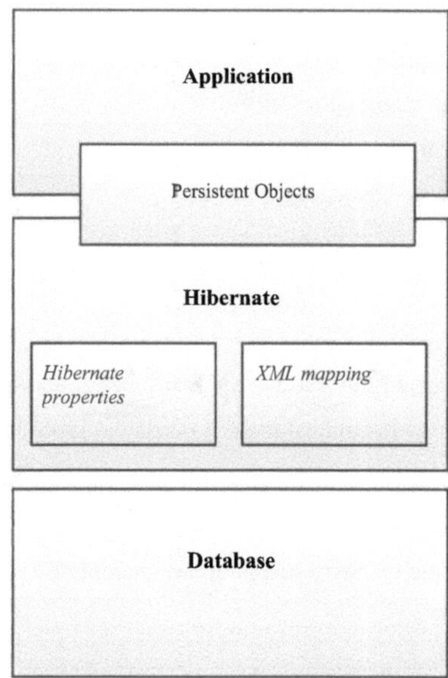

Figure 5 - Hibernate structure
Adapted from: Allapplabs, 2013

Figure 5 shows that there are three existing layers: Application, Hibernate and Database. As you can see, Hibernate performs these interconnections using its properties and XML mapping (ALLAPPLABS, 2013).

2.4.2 Frameworks

Frameworks that work with data persistence in any language must work independently of the application and the database. The persistence layer must mediate transactions between the data layer and the application. A good framework must offer data query capabilities, support and transactions, concurrency and also enable transparent persistence by encapsulating the relational database (COELHO; SARTORELLI, 2004).

Hibernate is a framework that relates to a database by doing all the processes related to object-relational mapping. Its purpose is to develop persistent classes in the Java language. Hibernate is known for its number of tools available to the developer and many features that facilitate programming and persistence as referenced by the website (ALLAPPLBS, 2013):

- Transparent persistence;
- Object-oriented query language;
- Object/relational mapping;
- Automatic primary key generation;
- High performance;
- J2EE integration.

2.4.3   Configured Hibernate

The configuration is carried out via the XML file itself, and in order to make a successful call to the database it is necessary to connect to each persistent layer and also to the linked mapping documents. You must specify the name of the data source or JDBC details that are required to make this connection to the database. The <session-factoy> element refers to the mapping that contains the domain object and Hibernate property mapping, an example of which can be seen in Figure 6 (ALLAPPLABS, 2013).

```
<DOCTYPE hibernate-configuration PUBLIC!
'-//Hibernate/Hibernate configuração DTD 3.0//EN"
'http://hibernate.sourceforge.net/hivernate-configuration-3.0.dtd">

<Hibernate-configuration>

    <session-factory>
        <property name="show_sql">true </property>
        <property name="hibernate.dialect">org.hibernate.dialect.MySQLMyISAMDialect </property>
        <property name="hibernate.connection.driver_class">org.gjt.mm.mysql.Driver </property>
        <property name="hibernate.connection.url">jdbc:mysql://localhost:3306/name </property>
        <property raiz name="hibernate.connection.username">username </property>
        <property name="hibernate.connection.password">password </property>

        <Mapping resource="org/name/hibernate/quickstart/name.hbm.xml"/>
    </Session-factory>
</Hibernate-configuration>
```

Figure 6 - Hibernate configuration file

Hibernate's configured properties are represented between <property> tags. These properties are responsible for making the connection with the DBMS and each of them has a specific background explained below according to (JBOSS, 2013).

- "Show_sql": Writes all SQL instructions to the console;
- "Hibernate.dialect": The name of a Hibernate class that allows you to generate optimized SQL for a particular relational database;
- "Hibernate.connection.driver_class": Driver specific to the bank being used, in the case of Figure 6 MySql;
- "Hibernate.connection.url": Defines and stores URL data for the bank's path;
- "Hibernate.connection.username": User who will access the database;
- "Hibernate.connection.password": Password of the user who will access the database.

The <mapping resourses> tag refers to the mapping document that contains the mapping of objects and classes in Hibernate.

2.4.4 Basic O/R mapping

Object-relational mapping can be defined in three approaches according to (JBOSS, 2013): using annotations through Java persistence, using JPA 2 XML which is the second JPA version or using an approach known as hbm.xml mapping through Hibernate's own XML.

The annotations are made so that Hibernate can control what is necessary for the links between the software and the database to be recognized, which is why objects, classes, entities and so on are annotated. The physical part of the database is represented by tables, columns, indexes and so on. The annotations are in the javax.persistence.* package, and their extensions are in org.hibernate.annotations.*. An example of mapping (Jboss, 2013).

```
1   package pojo;
2
3⊕ import javax.persistence.Column;
6
7   @Entity(name = "autores")
8   public class Autor {
9
10⊝     @Id
11      private int id;
12
13⊝     @Column (name = "nome")
14      private String nome;
15
16⊝     @Column (name = "contatoInfo")
17      private String contatoInfo;
18
19⊝     public int getId() {
20          return id;
21      }
22
23⊝     public void setId(int id) {
24          this.id = id;
25      }
26
27⊝     public String getNome() {
28          return nome;
29      }
30
31⊝     public void setNome(String nome) {
32          this.nome = nome;
33      }
34
35⊝     public String getContatoInfo() {
36          return contatoInfo;
37      }
38
```

Figure 7 - Example of a persistent class with Annotations.

The example in Figure 7 is of a Java persistent class, which is annotated with @Entity that Hibernate recognizes as an entity for the database. Other examples of the main annotations and their definitions are explained below (MARIANI, 2012):

- @Entity: Defines that the class will be recognized as an entity;
- @Table: Indicates the name of the table that Hibernate should look up in the database or generate. This annotation can be the same as the table relative to the one in the database;

- @Column: Defines several attributes, the main ones being the column name, size and value;
- @Id: Indicates the primary key of the database table;
- @GeneratedValue: This annotation defines the strategy for generating the identifiers, it will be set to AUTO, which lets the bank generate the values.

In addition to these, there are annotations to identify associations between tables in the database. To assign a "one-to-one" association, the @OneToOne annotation is used; for "many-to-one" associations, the @ManyToOne annotation is used.

2.5 NOSQL

This section will explain all the aspects of this model on the market, as well as various aspects of it.

2.5.1 NoSQL Definition

According to Lóscio et. Al, (2011) there is a large volume of data generated by web applications, these applications need requirements such as scalability on demand, degree of availability among other needs, with this new paradigms and technologies emerge.

Social networks are a good example cf managing large amounts of unstructured data, which is generated daily by millions of users.

In this context, a new NoSQL *(Not Cnly SQL)* concept emerged, which was proposed with the aim of meeting the requirements of managing large volumes of semi-structured or unstructured data. This new need arose from the large amount of data and the need for a non-relational database where queries can be faster (LÓSCIO; OLIVEIRA; PONTES, 2011).

These databases have been widely adopted in large technology companies such as Facebook, Twitter, Amazon, Digg, Linkedin and Google use NoSQL in some way. In addition, most NoSQL databases are open source and available as Cassandra, MongoDB, CouchDB, Redis, Riak, HBase and others.

2.5.2 History of NoSQL

Over the last 30 years, the relational model has been used in most systems. The first DBMSs were not based on relational structures but on hierarchical structures such as (IMS-DB) in the late 60s or graph-based (CODASYL - 70s). The relational model was only introduced by "Ted" Codd in the early 70s and was actually adopted in the late 80s. After the relational model was established and widely adopted, there were few alternatives to propose an alternative model and those that emerged were not very successful, such as object-oriented banks or xml banks (PORCELLI, 2012).

The NoSQL movement originated in June 2009, when Johan Oskarsson and Eric Evans held a meeting to discuss the emergence of Open Source solutions for distributed, non-relational data storage. In October of the same year, a "no:sql(east)" conference was held, which redefined some concepts about non-relational data storage solutions (PORCELLI, 2012).

In addition (Porcelli, 2012) writes that "it is important to understand that noSQL does not mean 'no SQL', but rather 'not only SQL'", which complements the meaning that NoSQL can also be a complement to the SQL language. The term was coined by (PORCELLI, 2012):

> "Apparently the term noSQL was coined in 1998 by Carlo Strozzi to name his open source project, which aimed to be a lighter implementation of a relational database, but its main feature was that it didn't expose the SQL interface."

After this important historical overview, you can delve deeper into NoSQL.

2.5.3   Characteristics of NoSQL Databases

NoSQL databases have fundamental characteristics that differentiate them from traditional databases, making them important for storing large volumes of unstructured or semi-structured data, according to (LÓSCIO, OLIVERIA, PONTES, 2011), some important characteristics can be mentioned:

- Absence of a flexible schema: An important feature of NoSQL databases is the complete or almost complete absence of the schema that defines the modeled data structure. This absence facilitates scalability and contributes to a greater increase in availability, so there is no guarantee of data integrity.

- Native Replication Support: Another way of providing scalability is through replication. There are two forms of replication: *Master-Slave*: each write results in a node. In this architecture, the write is done on the master node, and the write is redone on each slave node by the master. Reading becomes faster, but writing becomes slower. The other *Multi-Master:* In this case there are several master nodes, which reduces the bottleneck generated by writing.

- Simple API for data access: The aim of the NoSQL solution is to provide an efficient way of accessing data, offering high availability and scalability, the focus is not on how the data is stored but how we can retrieve it efficiently. APIs are developed to facilitate access to this information.

- Eventual consistency: This is a characteristic of NoSQL databases related to the fact that consistency cannot always be maintained between the various data distribution points. In the context of the Web, availability and partition tolerance are generally privileged, so ACID properties cannot be obeyed simultaneously. For this reason, there is another set of projects called BASE (Basically Available, Light State and Consistent at an Undetermined Time).

2.5.4 Scalability & Elasticity

According to (Porcelli, 2012) when we need to handle large volumes of data, we need to be able to create *clusters* not only for our application servers, but also for our tools.

Most relational database tools offer some horizontal scalability mechanism, but the relational model behaves better in a vertical scalability model (PORCELLI, 2012).

An important point when it comes to horizontal scalability (or clustering) is its elasticity, according to Porcelli (2012) on elasticity: *'the ability to "transparently" add new machines to the system - preferably without the need for remediation".*

Vertical and horizontal scalability are defined according to PORCELLI (2012):

> "Vertical scalability consists of adding more processing power, memory or disk to a machine, while horizontal scalability is the ability to add new machines to increase processing, memory and disk resources in a distributed way."

Vertical scalability has its simplicity, because initially it's easier to add more hardware without having to modify the software. However, at some point the cost of the hardware may become prohibitive or reach its limit. Horizontal scalability, on the other hand, has the greatest advantage of linear expansion, as it is always possible to add new machines, but working in a distributed way is much more complex (PORCELLI, 2012).

2.5.5 Implementation techniques

Some techniques are important for implementing NoSQL functionalities, as LÓSCIO, OLIVEIRA & PONTES (2011) state:

- *Map/reduce:* supports the management of large volumes of data distributed across the nodes of a network. In the map phase, problems are broken down into sub-problems that are distributed across several nodes in the network. In the reduce phase, the sub-problems are solved on each child node.

- *Consistent hashing:* Supports storage and retrieval mechanisms in distributed databases, where the number of sites is constantly changing.

- *Multiversion concurrency control (MVCC):* A mechanism that supports parallel transactions in a database. It allows read and write operations to be performed simultaneously.

- *Vector clocks:* These are used to generate an order of events that have occurred in a system. The use of an operation log with its dates is important for determining which version of a given piece of data is the most current.

2.5.6 Morphia framework for connecting to MongoDB (NoSQL)

The company 10gen, founder of MongoDB, provides a driver for accessing and manipulating the data in this database. This driver provides CRUD operations for the database (SOUZA, 2011).

According to Souza (2011), MongoDB was developed to persist data in the form of documents that are stored in collections. To speed up this data persistence programming, Google Code developed Morphia, an API that reduces complexity and increases developer productivity. One of Morphia's main advantages is the use of annotations in its classes for mapping.

The Morphia API uses the "com.mongodb.Mongo" class, which maintains an internal pool that controls through threads when to start and destroy an object. The integration between the Morphia API and the MongoDB driver is done through an object of the type "com.google.code.morphia.Datastore" (SOUZA, 2011).

The term mapping has been given to the way in which the entity classes of a Java application communicate with a persistence framework, whereby an attribute in the class refers to a field or column in the database. Using annotations, it is possible to indicate which class an object belongs to, create indexes, make references, create documents and so on. Some of the main annotations that Morphia uses and their definitions are as follows (SOUZA, 2011):

- @Embedded: A name is passed as a parameter, this key will be a field that you want to define, if no attribute name is entered, it will be used as the key.
- @Entitty: Defines an attribute. Creates the corresponding colleague that is annotated.
- @Proprierty: Used to change the name of a field in the document.
- @Reference: References a document saved in another folder.

All these annotations provided by Morphia make it easier to program and code the converter classes.

2.5.7 Data Model

Currently, the most widely used data model is the relational model, which is made up of tables, columns and rows and whose main characteristic is data integrity. However, the relational model is not always the most suitable for certain needs, such as hierarchical structures or dynamic structures. NoSQL tools include four types of data model: Key-Value, Document-Oriented, Column-Family and Graph according to Porcelli (2012).

2.5.7.1 Key-Value

Key-value oriented databases are databases where the system stores indexed values for retrieval by keys (BRITES, 2012).

The structure of the key-value model is for large pieces of information such as the blob data type, and everything is retrieved via the key, so the programmer has to be aware of this type of situation. Blob data type by Porcelli *(2012)· "A form of data storage without a defined structure that allows a large volume of data to be stored. "*. Some examples of key-value databases will be given in the following chapters.

2.5.7.2 Document

According to Porcelli (2012), "A document is a data structure made up of a variable number of fields with different data types, including a field that can contain another document (called a sub-document)."

You can imagine the documents as an XML or JSON file; in this model, there is no need to define their structure beforehand. These documents can be stored in the same structure or together without having anything in common. This is known as schema-free. Another characteristic of the document model is the tendency to denormalize data, leaving all related information in a single document (Porcelli, 2012).

An example of a document-oriented model can be seen in Figure 8.

```
 1   blog:{
 2       posts:{
 3           post:[{
 4               id: 1,
 5               nome: MEU POST!,
 6               texto: CONTEUDO DO POST,
 7               comentarios:{
 8                   [{
 9                       id: 1,
10                       usuario: anonimo,
11                       texto: Muito bom o post!
12                   }, {
13                       id: 2,
14                       usuario: anonimo,
15                       texto: Show de bola!
16                   }]
17                   }
18               }]
19           }
20   }
```

Figure 8 - Example of a JSON Format Document.

According to Lóscio et. Al (2011) the model stores collections of documents, this document is a unique identifier and a set of fields that can be strings, lists or nested documents. The JSON format is implemented using JavaScript.

2.5.7.2 Column family

The column family model became popular through the database created by Google *"BigTable"* in 2006. This database was designed with the aim of setting up a distributed data storage system with high performance, scalability and to support a large volume of data (PORCELLI, 2012).

According to Porcelli (2012), this model is made up of three components, Keyspaces, Column Families and Columns. The function of Keyspaces is to group together a set of Column Families. The Column Families component has the approximate structure of a relational model table, where data is stored in rows and columns. Finally, we have the Columns, which are the tuples where the data is actually stored. An example of a column family can be seen below in Figure 9.

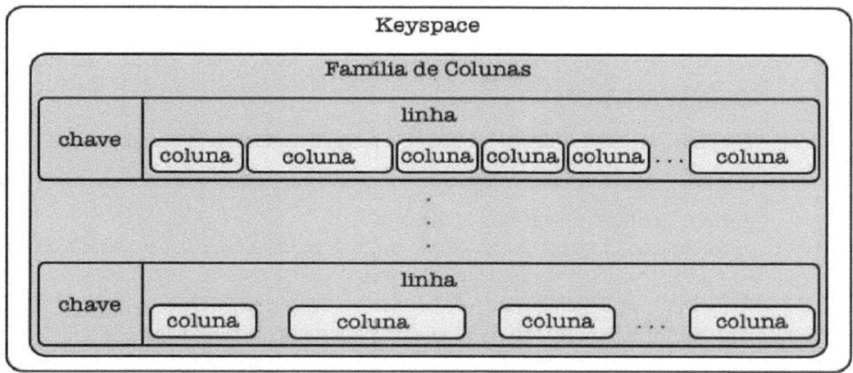

Figure 9 - Family cf Columns model (Porcelli, 2012)

Some examples of databases with the Column Family model will be described in the next chapters using HBase as an example.

2.5.7.3 Graph

A good description of the graph model comes from Marko Rodriguez (Graph Systems Architect at AT&T Interactive): "A graph is a data structure that connects a number of graphs. set of vertices via a set of edges. Modern graph databases support multi-relational graph structures, where there are different types of vertices (representing people, places, items) and different types of edges (e.g. friend of, lives in, bought by) [...] '.

According to Porcelli (2012), this model is the most natural for representing data, as we can create data in the same way that we draw elements connected by lines. A good example to represent this model is a social network, where people (who are represented by vertices) know or follow other people (relationships are represented by arrows of the type *Knows* or Follows*)*.

2.6 DATABASE FOR NOSQL

This section will describe databases with the data models that NOSQL supports.

2.6.1   Voldemort

Voldemort is a key-value storage system written in Java. Some features of the bank according to (VOLDEMORT, 2013):

- The data is divided between the servers and each contains a subset of the data;
- It allows signaling and integration with common frameworks such as Protocol Buffers, Thrift, Avro and Java Serialization;
- Each node is independent and has no central point;
- Read and write horizontally.

Linkedin uses it for certain scalability problems, high storage where space partitioning is not so simple and sufficient.

2.6.2   MongoDB

MongoDB is an open source database with a GPL *(General Public License)* for document-oriented storage. It is written in C++ and offered by the company 10gen (MONGODB, 2013).

"A colleague is a group of documents. If a document is a row in MongoDB compared to a row in a relational database, then a colleague can be thought of as a table" (CHORODOW; DIROLF, 2010).

According to Chorodow and Dirolf (2010), the Mongo bank has some characteristics such as:

- A document is the basic unit of data for MongoDB, equivalent to a row in a relational database;

- A collection is equivalent to a table;

- A single instance can host several independent databases, each with its own collections and permissions.

According to MongoDB, (2013) there are basic practices of risk management strategies such as:

- Vulnerability notification;
- Authentication;
- Data encryption;
- Access privileges.

This database also supports fault-tolerant replication and automatic recovery. Collections are made automatically via a shared key (CHORODOW; DIROLF, 2010).

The database also stores data in a JSON format as BSON binary. This file type supports any file type such as strings, float, integer and others (CATTEL, 2010).

(2011) MongoDB is a document-oriented database that can be used on different operating systems, such as Windows, Linux, OS X and Solaris. MongoDB also has drivers for various programming languages, including: C, C#, C++, Java, Perl, PHP, Python, Ruby.

The MongoDB data model is simple and can be described as follows (LÓSCIO; OLIVEIRA; PONTES, 2011):

- A **database** stores a set of collections;
- A **colleague** stores a set of documents;
- A **document** is a set of fields;
- A **field** is a key-value pair;
- A **key** is a name (string);
- A **value** is a character, integer, floating point, timestamp or binary. It can also be a document or an array of values.

2.6.3   HBase

According to Cattell (2010), HBase is an Apache project written in Java and has some basic characteristics:

- Uses a distributed file system;
- Line operations are atomic;
- The files are compressed;
- Java Client API;
- MapReduce, great processing.

The purpose of HBase is to host very large tables (Billions of rows x Millions of columns). Row operations are atomic, with locks and transitions (HBASE, 2013).

2.6.4   InfoGrid

InfoGrid is a Client/Server system for environments with a large computing capacity. It also supports the use and management of distributed computing resources and offers many facilities for integrating and managing data and users (BRITES, 2012).

The graph database contains nodes and edges. Nodes are independent objects in a graph database, edges are objects that depend on other objects and edges are used to make connections between nodes (BRITES, 2012).

Edges do not exist in normal code; almost all languages contain pointers. Edges are bidirectional and can be controlled (BRITES, 2012).

2.6.5   Success stories

According to Lóscio, Oliveira and Pontes (2011), NoSQL technology has become increasingly evident in recent years, as evidenced by the strong adoption of NoSQL solutions in large companies for data management such as:

- **Twiter:** Twiter is a social network and server for microblogging. With the exponential growth of this network, solving problems of accessing large volumes of data in real time has become a major challenge. In February 2010, the number of Tweets was 1.2 billion per month. The scalability problem led the company to replace its MySQL database with Cassandra. The company uses Cassandra to store *data mining* results from its user base, *trend topics*, *@toptweets* and large-scale real-time analysis.

- **Facebook:** Six years after its creation, Facebook currently has around 3.5 billion pieces of content (links, posts, etc.) shared every week. To avoid problems with availability and scalability, the company developed Cassandra (NoSQL). Initially created to optimize Facebook, Cassandra is now used to support replication, fault detection and other functionalities. It is also used by other companies such as Cisco, Digg and Twiter.

- **Google:** Google has also developed its NoSQL solution, called BigTable, which is a distributed storage system for managing large-scale structured data. This solution allows scalability of resources, as well as high performance in the processing of queries, processes and services.

- **Amazon:** One of the major challenges faced by Amazon.com concerns the reliability of the large volume of data managed by its applications. In 2007, in order to guarantee high availability of the data on its services, Amazon developed a NoSQL solution, Dynamo. This has ensured that 99.9995% of requests are available.

- **Linkedin:** Linkedin is a business network, founded in 2002, which focuses on establishing professional relationships. To meet the demands of its applications, it developed its own NoSQL-based solution, called Voldemort, which has produced excellent results. Voldemort supports horizontal scalability, replication, partitioning, fault transparency and other features.

3   MATERIALS AND METHODS

This section will present the materials, methods and configuration needed to develop an application for comparing Relational and Non-Relational structures.

3.1 DATABASES AND FRAMEWORKS USED

To implement the application with a relational database, it is necessary to configure the MySQL database available for download at http://www.mysql.com/downloads/ and the Hibernate framework available at (http://www.hibernate.org/downloads).

To implement the application with a non-relational, document-oriented database, we used the NoSQL MongoDB database available for download at (http://www.mongodb.org/downloads) and the Morphia persistence framework available for download at (https://code.google.com/p/morphia/downloads/list).

3.2   PROGRAMMING TOOLS

Other tools were also used to program the application, such as the Eclipse IDE, available for download at http://www.eclipse.org/downloads/.

The language used was Java, available for download at (http://www.oracle.com/technetwork/java/javase/downloads/index .html).

4 EXPERIMENTAL STUDY

To illustrate the concepts discussed, an example of creating an application using the Java language and the MySQL relational database will be presented, as well as the same application but using the MongoDB non-relational database (NoSQL).

4.1 DESCRIPTION OF THE APPLICATION

As a case study, an application is developed for a bookstore. Author, publisher, book and contact information will be entered. In this context, each item will be persisted in these databases.

4.2 APPLICATION

This section will show the class diagram, demonstrating the basic application, as well as the ER diagram.

The class diagram represents a real-world entity, process or concept that has identity, attributes and behavior Silva (2013). This conceptual model was applied to the model that will be developed in both databases, as shown in Figure 10, the basic concept of a bookstore.

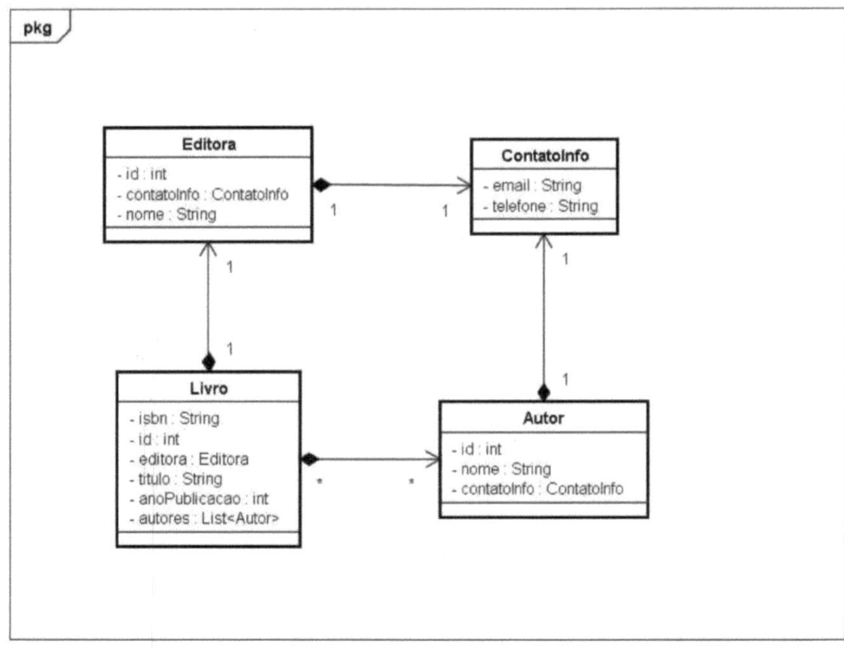

Figure 10 - Bookshop Class Diagram

The entity-relationship modeling (ERM) diagram developed with MySQL Workbench can be seen in Figure 11.

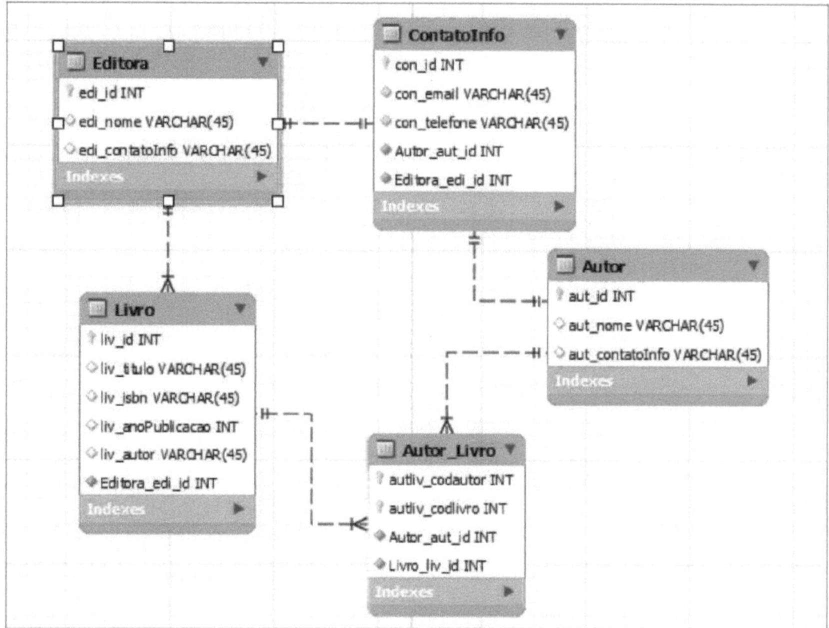

Figure 11 - MER Bookstore

From these logical models (MER) and class diagrams we can build a relational database. In the NoSQL paradigm, none of these artifacts are used because, as we saw during development, NoSQL is free of this schema and does not require a previous structure.

4.3 POJO, MAPPING WITH HIBERNATE AND MYSQL

The POJO package was created for the bookstore application. In this package, the classes that refer to the bookstore project were created, which are represented by the Author, ContactInfo, Publisher and Book classes.

These classes are mapped using JPA *(Java Persistence API)* annotations, which is an API *(Application Programming Interface)* of the Java language and is used to persist data in any database. Within this context, the JPA creates a "persistence.xml" file which is where the connections to the database are mapped.

In the persistence file, the connections and drivers are configured, in this case using the

MySQL driver as the database and its respective classes, along with the user, password and url as shown in Figure 12.

```xml
 1  <?xml version="1.0" encoding="UTF-8"?>
 2  <persistence version="2.0"
 3      xmlns="http://java.sun.com/xml/ns/persistence" xmlrs:xsi="http://www.w3.org/2001/XMLSchema-instance"
 4      xsi:schemaLocation="http://java.sun.com/xml/ns/persistence http://java.sun.com/xml/ns/persistence/persistence_2_0.xsd">
 5      <persistence-unit name="PosHibernate">
 6          <class>pojo.Autor</class>
 7          <class>pojo.ContatoInfo</class>
 8          <class>pojo.Editora</class>
 9          <class>pojo.Livro</class>
10
11
12
13          <properties>
14              <property name="javax.persistence.jdbc.url" value="jdbc:mysql://localhost:3306/hibernate" />
15              <property name="javax.persistence.jdbc.user" value="root" />
16              <property name="javax.persistence.jdbc.password" value="" />
17              <property name="javax.persistence.jdbc.driver" value="com.mysql.jdbc.Driver" />
18          </properties>
19
20
21      </persistence-unit>
22  </persistence>
```

Figure 12 - Persistence.xml file

The annotations are part of Figure 13, which shows the main annotations for mapping in the database.

```java
 1  package pojo;
 2
 3  import javax.persistence.Column;
 6
 7  @Entity(name = "autores")
 8  public class Autor {
 9
10      @Id
11      private int id;
12
13      @Column (name = "nome")
14      private String nome;
15
16      @Column (name = "contatoInfo")
17      private String contatoInfo;
18
19      public int getId() {
20          return id;
21      }
22
23      public void setId(int id) {
24          this.id = id;
25      }
26
27      public String getNome() {
28          return nome;
29      }
```

Figure 13 - Mapping with Anotares

The *@Entity, @Id, @Column* annotations show Hibernate that these objects will be mapped in the database with their respective names.

4.4   DAO PACKAGE

The DAO *(Data Access Object)* package is a persistence standard for mapping objects and executing SQL commands, as well as CRUD operations on the database. Figure 14 shows the code for saving an Author in the database.

```
 1  package dao;
 2
 3  import javax.persistence.EntityManager;
 6
 7  public class AutorDAO {
 8
 9      public AutorDAO() {
10          // TODO Auto-generated constructor stub
11      }
12
13      protected EntityManager em;
14
15      public AutorDAO(EntityManager em) {
16          this.em = em;
17      }
18
19      public Autor createAutor(int id, String nome, String contatoInfo) {
20          Autor aut = new Autor();
21          aut.setId(id);
22          aut.setNome(nome);
23          aut.setContatoInfo(contatoInfo);
24          em.persist(aut);
25          return aut;
26
27      }
```

Figure 14 - AuthorDAO

4.5   POJO, MAPPING WITH MORPHIA AND MONGODB

Morphia is an API from Google. This API can be added to the project to map the objects to the database, in this case MongoDB. The project structure is the same as the previous one, changing only a few aspects such as annotations.

The POJO can be identified in the same way as in the relational project, but with different annotations, as Morphia is used here. This can be seen in the different annotations in Figure 15.

```
 1  package pojo;
 2
 3⊕ import java.io.Serializable;⎕
12
13  @Entity("autores")
14  public class Autor implements Serializable {
15
16⊖      /**
17       *
18       */
19      private static final long serialVersionUID = 1L;
20
21⊖      @Id
22      private ObjectId id;
23
24⊖      @Indexed(value = IndexDirection.ASC, name = "idxAutor", unique = true)
25      private String nome;
26
27⊖      @Embedded("info")
28      private ContatoInfo contatoInfo;
29
30⊖      public ObjectId getId() {
31          return id;
32      }
```

Figure 15 - Pojo with Morphia

You can see the differences in the annotations *@Indexed* defines that a field will be an index while *@Embedded is* used as a key.

4.6   DAO CLASSES, CONNECTION CLASSES

The DAO package can be seen with the same classes in the relational project, but there are differences, as the Morphia API offers a basic DAO (CRUD operations), already in the API itself. Example of basic DAO shown in Figure 16.

```
 1  package dao;
 2
 3⊕ import org.bson.types.ObjectId;
.0
.1  public class AutorDAO extends BasicDAO<Autor, ObjectId>{
.2
.3⊖      public AutorDAO(Datastore datastore) {
.4          super(datastore);
.5          ensureIndexes();
.6      }
.7
.8  }
.9
```

Figure 16 - DAO Morphia

This DAO performs basic CRUD operations. Figure 17 shows code from the ConnectionMorphia class, which the Morphia framework uses to connect to MongoDB.

```
 1  package dao;
 2
 3⊕ import java.net.UnknownHostException;⬚
 8
 9  public class MorphiaConnection {
10
11      private static final String DB_HOST = "127.0.0.1";
12      private static final String DB_NAME = "morphia";
13
14      private static MorphiaConnection connection;
15      private Mongo mongo;
16
17      private Datastore catastore;
18  |
19⊖     public MorphiaConnection() {
20          super();
21      }
22
23⊖     public static MorphiaConnection getInstance() {
24          if (connection == null) {
25              connection = new MorphiaConnection();
26          }
27          return connection;
28      }
29
30⊖     private Mongo mongoDB() {
31          if (mongo == null) {
32              try {
33                  mongo = new Mongo(DB_HOST);
34              } catch (UnknownHostException e) {
35                  e.printStackTrace();
36              }
```

Figure 17 - Morphia and MongoDB connection

You can see that lines 11 and 12 are creating variables and receiving the default value for the local connection to MongoDB. Two MorphiaConnection and MongoDB methods are also created. These methods generate interactions between all the project's methods and objects and the database.

4.4   RESULTS AND CONCLUSIONS

During the construction of the work, it can be seen that both structures that have been described are similar, only the annotations, frameworks used and the way of recording are different.

No performance comparisons were made between the structures. The main effect of the comparison to be noted is that the write structures are different in the respective databases, using alternative ways of writing data to disk in each relational/non-relational structure.

Another important part to mention is that vertical and horizontal scalability are different in each bank. In the NOSQL context, there is no need to invest heavily in order to have a suitable structure, which, unlike the vertical structure used by relational banks, is sometimes expensive.

5   FINAL CONSIDERATIONS

This chapter presents the conclusion of the work carried out, as well as what can be done in the future in relation to it.

5.1 CONCLUSION

By comparing the structures of the two types of database (MySQL and MongoDB) using an application for comparison with the tools of each type of database, it was possible to verify that the main difference between one structure and the other is the way in which it is recorded. There was also the introduction of important concepts about these new market technologies applied and that there is still significant learning in relation to what can be achieved innovatively using a mixture of tools.

In terms of general structure, NoSQL offers more advantages over relational structures because its growth can be horizontal, not limited to the growth of the application in terms of software and hardware invested, while the vertical structure used with relational banks has a much higher cost.

The mappings and structure of the project itself haven't changed much, only some annotations and methods are different in the NoSQL structure.

5.2 FUTURE WORK/CONTINUATION OF WORK

This project could be implemented again, testing new features and also the performance of each tool by comparing the two. Also the use of NoSQL technologies on the market in terms of performance and productivity.

BIBLIOGRAPHICAL REFERENCES

ALLAPPLABS. **HIBERNATE - Introduction to Hibernate.** Available at:
<http://www.allapplabs.com/hibernate/introduction_to_hibernate.htm>. Accessed on: February 28,
2013.

BRITES, C. M. **Database NOSQL Concepts and Applicability**. Novo Hamburgo,
2 012.

CATTELL, R. **Scalable SQL and NoSQL Data Store.** ACM SIGMOD Record, pp. 12-27,
(December 04, 2010).

CHORODOW, K., & DIROLF, M. **MongoDB. The Definitive Guide.** USA: O'Reilly Media,
2010.

COELHO and SARTORELLI, C. A. **Persistence of Objects.** Sao Paulo, 2004.

COUCHDB. **CouchDB**. Available at: <http://couchdb.apache.org/>. Accessed on: March 20. 2013.

GOOGLE. S.D. **Bigtable: A Distributed Storage System for Structured Data**. Available
at:<http://static.googleusercontent.com/external_content/untrusted_dlcp/research.google.co m/en-
BR//archive/bigtable-osdi06.pdf>. Accessed on: March 21. 2013.

HBASE. **Hbase**. Available at Hbase:
<http://hbase.apache.org/book/architecture.html#arch.overview>. Accessed on: March 21.
2 013.

HEUSER, C. A. **Database Project.** Porto Alegre, Ed. Sagra Luzzatto, 2004.

IMASTERS. **The importance of scalability for your company's growth.**
Available from <http://imasters.com.br/artigo/17099/gerencia-de-ti/a-importancia-da-
scalability-for-the-growth-of-your-company/> Accessed on March 04, 2013. 2013.

JBOSS. HIBERNATE - **Relational Persistence for Idiomatic Java.** Available at:
<http://docs.jboss.org/hibernate/core/3.5/reference/pt-BR/pdf/hibernate_reference.pdf> Accessed
on: March 07. 2013.

KORTH, H. F. **Database Systems.** Sao Paulo: Pearson Makron Books, 1999.

LÓSCIO, B. F. OLIVEIRA, H. R., & PONTES, J. C. (March 15, 2011). **NoSQL in the
development of collaborative web applications.** VIII SBSC.

MACHADO E ABREU, F. N. **Projeto de Banco de Dados.** Sao Paulo: Érica, 2004.

MARIANI, T. **Use of Frameworks for Relational Object Mapping and a comparative analysis
with non-relational databases.** UTFPR, Medianeira.

MONGODB. **MongoDB**. Available at MongoDB: <http://www.mongodb.org/>. Accessed on:
March 20. 2013.

MYSQL. **What is MySQL?** Available at: <http://dev.mysql.com/doc/refman/5.6/en/what-is.html>. Accessed on: March 28. 2013.

ORACLE.   **Products**. Available at: <http://www.oracle.com/br/products/index.html>. Accessed on: 04 de Margo. 2013.

ORACLE. **Oracle Company.** Available at: <http://www.mysql.com/products/workbench/>. Accessed on: February 26, 2013.

PORCELLI, A. (2012**). What is NoSQL? An overview of the buzzword of the moment - Part 1.** DevMedia, 21-30.

Roman et al, E. **Mastering Enterprise JavaBeans**. Sao Paulo: BookMan, 2002.

SILVIA,   R,   V.   **Class Diagram**   .   Available at   :   <http://www.inf.ufpr.br/silvia/ESNovo/UML/pdf/ModeloConceitualAl.pdf>. Accessed on: March 03. 2013.

SILVA E OLIVEIRA, I. J. (2005). **Database.** Rio de Janeiro: Alta Books Ltda, 2005.

SOUZA, M. B. (2011). **Introducing the Morphia API.** DevMedia, 11-18.

VOLDEMORT. **Project Voldemort.** Available at Project Voldemort: <http://www.project-voldemort.com/voldemort/>. Accessed on: March 10. 2013.